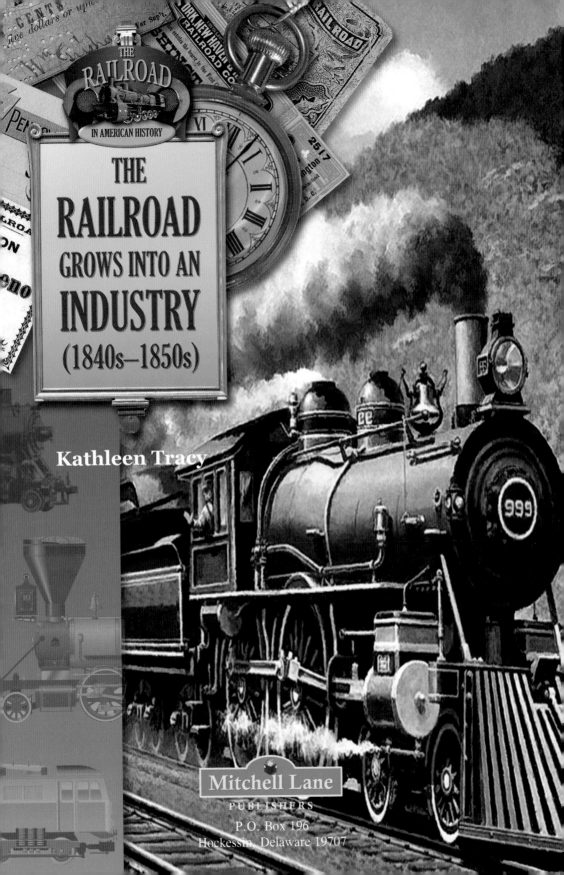

THE RAILROAD
IN AMERICAN HISTORY

THE
RAILROAD
GROWS INTO AN
INDUSTRY
(1840s–1850s)

Kathleen Tracy

Mitchell Lane
PUBLISHERS
P.O. Box 196
Hockessin, Delaware 19707

THE RAILROAD
IN AMERICAN HISTORY

The Birth of the Locomotive
The Railroad Comes to America
The Railroad Grows into an Industry
The Railroad and the Civil War
The Railroad Fuels Westward Expansion
Electric Trains and Trolleys

The publisher would like to thank Milton C. Hallberg for acting as a consultant on its *The Railroad in American History* series. He is a professor emeritus of agricultural economics at Pennsylvania State University and has been a visiting professor at universities around the world. His railroad interests began when he attended a railroad telegraphers' school in preparation for a job as a depot agent on the CB&Q Railroad in Illinois. After retiring from teaching, he returned to his railroad interests as a new hobby, during which time he has written about early rail systems.

PUBLISHER'S NOTE:
The facts on which this book is based have been thoroughly researched. Documentation of such research can be found on page 44. While every possible effort has been made to ensure accuracy, the publisher will not assume liability for damages caused by inaccuracies in the data, and makes no warranty on the accuracy of the information contained herein.

Printing
1 2 3 4 5 6 7 8 9

Library of Congress Cataloging-in-Publication Data
Tracy, Kathleen.
The railroad grows into an industry (1840–1850) / by Kathleen Tracy.
    p. cm. —(The railroad in American history)
Includes bibliographical references and index.
ISBN 978-1-61228-288-6 (library bound)
1. Railroads—United States—History—Juvenile literature. 2. Railroads and state--United States—History—Juvenile literature. I. Title.
HE2751.T69 2013
385.0973'09034—dc23
                                        2012009426

eBook ISBN: 9781612283623

PLB

CONTENTS

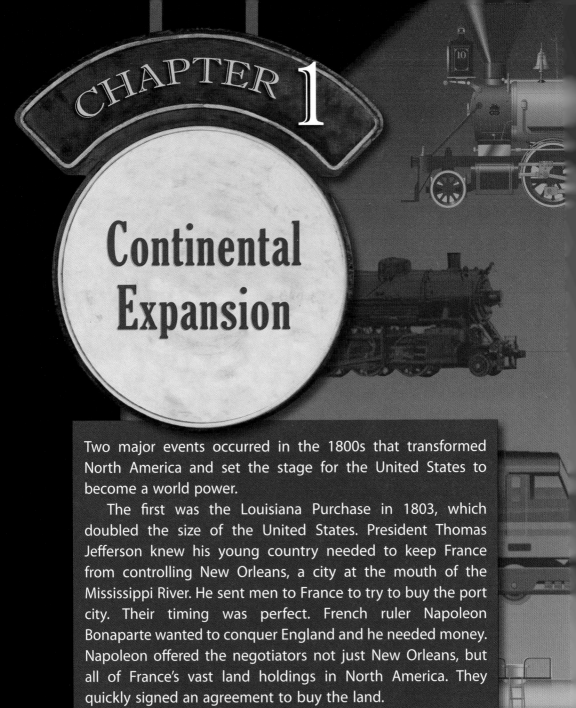

CHAPTER 1

Continental Expansion

Two major events occurred in the 1800s that transformed North America and set the stage for the United States to become a world power.

The first was the Louisiana Purchase in 1803, which doubled the size of the United States. President Thomas Jefferson knew his young country needed to keep France from controlling New Orleans, a city at the mouth of the Mississippi River. He sent men to France to try to buy the port city. Their timing was perfect. French ruler Napoleon Bonaparte wanted to conquer England and he needed money. Napoleon offered the negotiators not just New Orleans, but all of France's vast land holdings in North America. They quickly signed an agreement to buy the land.

The Louisiana Purchase spanned from the Mississippi River to the Rocky Mountains. It stretched from New Orleans all the way north to what would become Canada. It included all or parts of what would become fifteen states: Arkansas, Colorado, Iowa, Kansas, Louisiana, Minnesota, Missouri, Montana,

The United States flag was first raised in New Orleans on March 10, 1804 to commemorate Louisiana becoming an American territory.

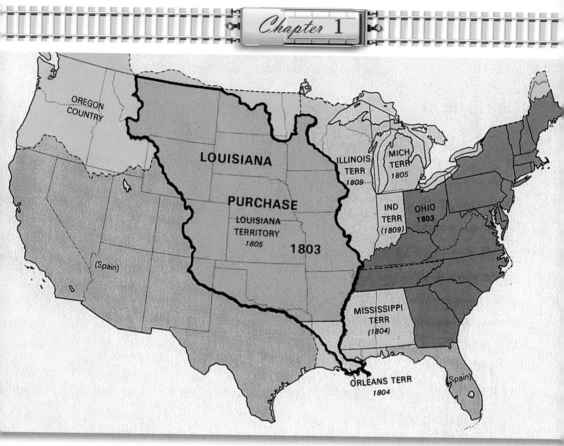

The Louisiana Purchase

Nebraska, New Mexico, North Dakota, Oklahoma, South Dakota, Texas, and Wyoming.

The huge swath of land—828,000 square miles (2.1 million square kilometers)—was bought for only $15 million, which came to less than five cents an acre.

The second major event took place in 1846, when the Unites States went to war against Mexico. At the time, Mexico controlled a vast area of what is now the American West. Mexico had claimed the land after its war for independence from Spain. The Republic of Texas declared its own independence in 1836, but Mexico ignored this move. Nine years later, in 1845, Texas became part of the United States. Mexico viewed this as theft. It had never recognized Texas' independence, and it still considered the land part of Mexico.

The Mexican-American War began with the bloody and brutal Battle of Palo Alto in May 1846. It ended a year and a half later with the Treaty

of Guadalupe Hidalgo, signed on February 2, 1848. As part of the treaty's terms, the United States acquired more than 500,000 square miles (1.3 million square kilometers) of territory. The area spanned from the Rocky Mountains to the Pacific coast, and north to the border of today's Oregon.

Gaining these two huge chunks of land fulfilled the idea of America's Manifest Destiny. This was the belief some people held that the United States had a right to take over the land between the Atlantic and the Pacific. Controlling all the resources from sea to shining sea would be a huge economic and political boon to the young country.

Early Railroads

In 1826, the Granite Railway opened in Massachusetts to haul granite from a quarry in Quincy to the Neponset River. It went on to become one of the country's first common carriers, carrying passengers and freight for whoever was willing to pay. More and more local and regional railroads began to crisscross the eastern states. Most early rail projects were for short freight or passenger lines. States gave them charters without establishing any oversight for their construction, or worrying about whether they would eventually connect with other railroads.

However, as the U.S. economy and population grew, it became clear that there was a need for a network of railroads that would link cities and businesses. The sheer size of America made it hard for people to travel by wagon or horseback. Businesses that wanted to sell their goods across the country needed a better, faster way. As a result, in the decades leading up to the Civil War, railroads evolved into a powerful industry that helped shape the country's economic, social, and political development.

Before a true railroad network could be built, the government needed to know exactly what it owned and how best to use it. Its land needed to be accurately surveyed and mapped. In the years immediately following the Louisiana Purchase, most mapping was conducted informally by the United States military in sparsely populated territories. The government was mostly concerned with finding easy routes for soldiers to travel along. They also wanted maps to help establish state and territory boundaries. As a result, the maps produced were not very detailed.

Early railroad surveys were paid for by private investors. The first important railroad map publishing house was started by Joseph Hutchins Colton. Born in Longmeadow, Massachusetts, Colton moved to New York in 1831 to pursue his career as a cartographer, or mapmaker. In the early years of his business, Colton bought the copyrights of previously published maps and reproduced them, using engraved steel plates, which produced higher quality prints. Older maps were typically made using wax engravings. Colton's maps were also hand painted with watercolors, and he gave them a distinctive decorative border. Later in his career, Colton was hired to create original maps based on new surveys.

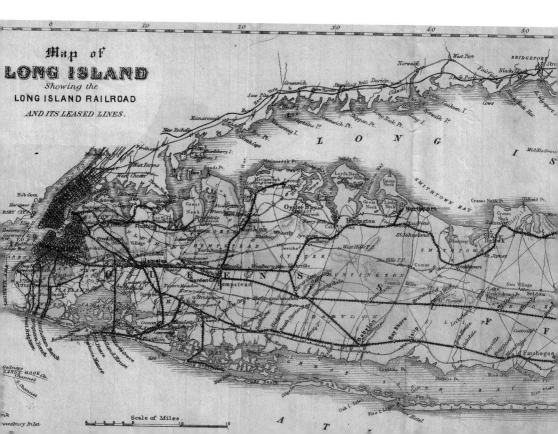

Throughout the 1840s and 1850s, the government sent surveying and mapping excursions to many areas. John Charles Fremont became known as the "Pathfinder" for leading surveys to the Rocky Mountains, Oregon, and California. A survey of the border between the United States and Mexico took place between 1848 and 1855, and other excursions were organized to map the boundaries of Texas and Florida.

The movement to link all corners of America by railroads gained strength among business leaders and politicians. The idea of a railroad that ran from the Atlantic to the Pacific coast was especially intriguing. Lawmakers disagreed about the route such a railroad should take—northern states did not want a southern route and southern states didn't want a northern route. But with California prospering thanks to the discovery of gold in 1848, the business opportunities were too big to ignore.

Competition was fierce among businessmen and politicians over what route would be used. The areas the railroad passed through

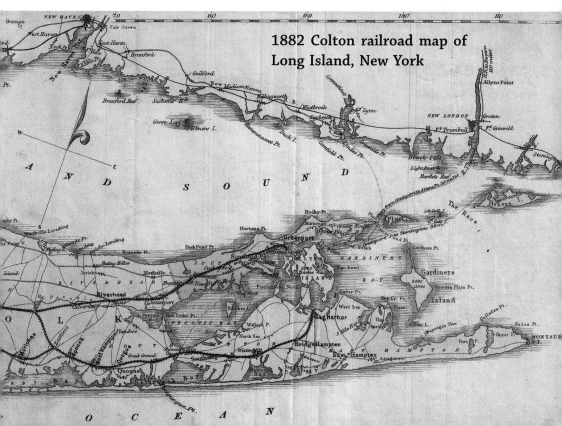

1882 Colton railroad map of Long Island, New York

Left: A scene from a Whipple exploration

would enjoy huge business and financial benefits. What the government cared most about was keeping costs down. The cost to build a railroad to the West Coast would equal the entire federal budget for a year.

In 1853, Congress ordered the Army Corps of Topographical Engineers to determine the most practical and least expensive route for a railroad from the Mississippi River to the Pacific Ocean. Four potential east-west routes would be surveyed.

Isaac Stephens led the Northern Pacific expedition through Minnesota, North Dakota, Montana, Idaho, Washington, and Oregon.

John Gunnison led the Central Pacific expedition, starting in St. Louis, passing through Kansas, Colorado, Utah, and Nevada, and ending in San Francisco, California.

Amiel Whipple, who had previously surveyed the U.S.-Mexican border, led a Southern Pacific expedition from Albuquerque, New Mexico, through Arizona and into Los Angeles, California. John Parke and John Pope led another Southern Pacific expedition, close to the Mexican border.

After years of surveying, Congress finally agreed on a route and in 1862 members passed the first Pacific Railroad Act. It was decided that the Union Pacific Railroad would build tracks starting in Omaha, Nebraska, and heading west. The Central Pacific would start laying track in Sacramento, California, and head east. On May 10, 1869, the two railroads met at Promontory Summit in Utah, officially creating the first transcontinental railroad. Together, the railroad companies laid 1,774 miles (2,855 kilometers) of track. Other transcontinental lines followed.

Before that, in the 1840s and the 1850s, steam locomotives became the primary muscle behind moving America's freight. Railroads became one of the most valuable industries in the world, and they often turned their owners into millionaires and power brokers of the Industrial Revolution.

Corps of Topographical Engineers

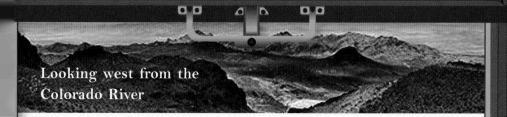

Looking west from the
Colorado River

Members of the U.S. Army's Corps of Topographical Engineers were the unsung heroes in charting the American West. They spent long periods of time away from friends and family, and risked their health and even their lives to create maps that led to roads and rail lines to the California coast.

Congress created the corps in 1838. The surveying and mapping of the West was expected to help the government maintain military control, identify natural resources, and choose the best routes for transportation. The Topogs, as they were known, led teams that often included artists and scientists, who made notes and drawings of everything they saw.

Their expeditions literally went into uncharted territory. For example, in September 1851, Captain Lorenzo Sitgreaves was sent to map the Zuni and Colorado rivers and report on whether they could be navigated. Although the army was aware there was a canyon located somewhere along the Colorado River, few members imagined just how big the Grand Canyon would prove to be.

The Topogs endured great physical discomfort. They spent nearly every waking hour riding horses. There were nights when they had to sleep on the hard ground. When they bathed, it was in cold river water. Trail food was largely salted pork, a kind of cracker called hardtack, and whatever fish or game they could catch or hunt. Sometimes even that food ran out, and members of one expedition were forced to kill and eat their pack mules. They also faced harsh weather, venomous snakes, and Native Americans who were starting to fight back against increasing expansion into their homelands. The Corps of Topographical Engineers was merged with the Army Corps of Engineers in March 1863 during the Civil War.

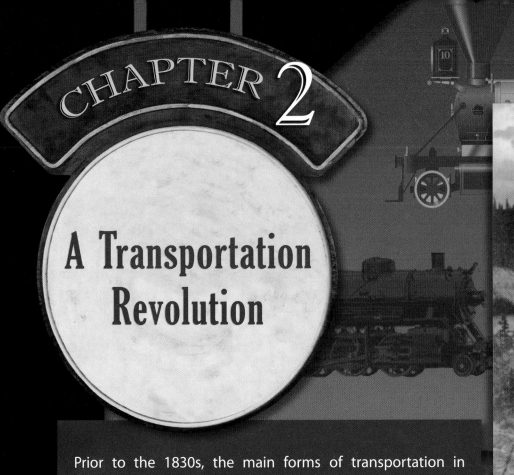

CHAPTER 2

A Transportation Revolution

Prior to the 1830s, the main forms of transportation in America were wagons and steamboats. Developed in the early 1800s, steamboats quickly became the primary way of moving large quantities of freight and passengers. When the first railroads were built, they were seen as a novelty. However, once they proved successful, steamboat and stagecoach company owners started seeing them as a threat. They didn't want more railroads to be built.

It wasn't just direct competitors who were against railroads. Innkeepers and other business owners along stagecoach and steamboat routes worried that their livelihoods could be harmed. Fewer travelers meant fewer people to buy a meal or rent a room for the night. Even some religious leaders got involved, claiming that trains were unholy. Some doctors warned that traveling at high speeds was dangerous to the human body.

A steamboat on the Yukon River

Despite those worries, the practical and economic advantages of trains were too big to be denied. For example, taking a steamboat from Cincinnati to St. Louis took three days; taking a train took just sixteen hours. In addition to going faster, trains could take a more direct route. The steamboat from Cincinnati traveled 702 miles (1,130 kilometers) while the train covered only 339 miles (546 kilometers).

In the East, using boats to travel along rivers, canals, and lakes worked well. But as more and more people pushed westward, the greater distances proved challenging. The Mississippi and Ohio rivers were great transportation waterways to cities on their banks and to the Gulf of Mexico. However, developing a more efficient means of transportation for the vast inland areas of America was crucial to the country's industrial and economic growth.

Up until the start of the nineteenth century, the United States was mostly a farming nation, with less emphasis placed on manufacturing. Farmers were highly self-sufficient and made most of the tools they needed. Early Americans prided themselves on their ingenuity. The country as a whole, though, was slow to rush headlong into the Industrial Revolution, which started in Europe in the late 1700s. In the United States, economic growth was based on a few industries, including shipbuilding, and on commerce such as cotton sales.

By the early 1800s, in order to keep up with the rest of the world, the United States had no choice but to embrace industrialization. Once its workers did, American innovation advanced many industries. According to historian Henry J. Sage, "In America, individual freedom encouraged resourcefulness and experimentation, business growth encouraged new techniques, and the chronic labor shortage encouraged the substitution of machinery. Even the British admired American inventiveness."[1] That inventiveness and innovation would transform the railroad industry.

The earliest railroads were simply horse-drawn wagons that ran along wooden rails. It was crude, but it worked much better than pulling wagons along uneven ground. However, horses moved slowly

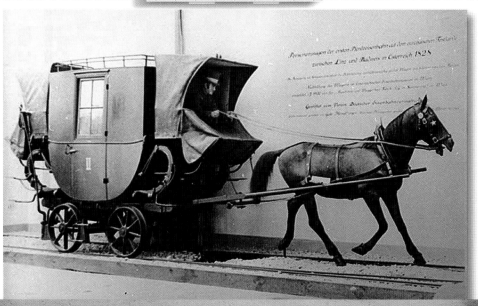

The first horse-drawn train was introduced on September 7, 1827, in Czechoslovakia.

and could only pull limited amounts of goods. They got tired and hungry, and needed to rest and eat. A mechanical solution was needed.

One of the most important innovations for the railroad industry was the development of the locomotive steam engine. In 1804, an English mining engineer named Richard Trevithick built a steam locomotive that was capable of hauling wagons carrying as much as ten tons of iron. His engine had one cylinder, a horizontal boiler, and four driving wheels. It reached speeds of up to five miles (eight kilometers) per hour on tracks between the Penydarren Ironworks and a canal in Wales. Other English engineers, like George Stephenson and Matthew Murray, were also building early locomotives.

By 1829, the first English-designed steam locomotives went into service in America. The huge engines worked well on England's straight, flat iron tracks, but they were too heavy for the United States' strap-iron rails—made of wood and capped with a thin layer of iron. English

The *Tom Thumb*

locomotives were also too big to make sharp curves or zip up steep hills.

The problem was solved by businessman and inventor Peter Cooper, who developed America's first steam locomotive. Cooper worked for a carriage maker, and went on to own furniture and glue factories and an iron foundry. When the Baltimore and Ohio Railroad was established in 1827, Cooper invested a lot of money in land around Baltimore. The ultimate goal of the B&O Railroad was to connect Baltimore to the Ohio River. By 1829, only thirteen miles (twenty-one kilometers) of track was being serviced by horse-drawn wagons. The cost for renting the horses was $33 a day, an exorbitant sum at the time.

Cooper decided to build a locomotive that could help the company—and his investment. Cooper's steam engine had an upright boiler that was around five feet (one and a half meters) tall and used two old musket barrels for pipes. It was fueled by coal that heated water in the boiler. To make the coal burn hot so it would create enough steam, he connected a blower to a drum, which was attached to one of the locomotive's wheels.

Called *Tom Thumb* because of its small size, the locomotive was ready for its debut on August 28, 1830. Cooper acted as engineer and thirty-six passengers—railroad dignitaries and their friends—filled an open-air carriage behind the locomotive. *Tom Thumb* successfully traveled the thirteen miles between Baltimore and Ellicott's Mills in just seventy-two minutes, easily navigating sharp turns and hills.

The railroad executives were convinced that steam power was the future of the B&O, and the following year they held a contest for the best locomotive—with a $4,000 prize for the winner. Watchmaker Phineas Davis won with his locomotive, called the *York*. It was able to handle curves at fifteen miles (twenty-four kilometers) per hour, and easily reached speeds of thirty miles (forty-eight kilometers) per hour on a straightaway. Most important, it cost just $16 to run the *York* all day, half the cost of using horses.

The *York*

The agility of engines like the *York* and others built in America was due to an improved design over British models. Instead of building locomotives on a rigid frame that extended outside the wheels, American designers put the frame inside the wheels, making them much lighter and more flexible. It also made them more durable, meaning they needed fewer repairs.

Stopping early trains was a difficult task. Brakemen had to stop the train by jumping from car to car and setting handbrakes on each one. It was a time-consuming and dangerous process. The brakemen responded to whistle signals by the engineer, and if they didn't hear the signals, the train might not stop in time to avoid a collision. The handbrakes couldn't always control a train going down a steep hill, and runaway trains were known to fly off the rails.

In 1869, George Westinghouse introduced a brake that used compressed air to force the brake shoes against the train wheels. He went on to make many improvements to the system, making trains much safer and able to travel at higher speeds.

The most commonly used classification of locomotives is called the Whyte notation, after Frederick Whyte, who devised the system in the early 1900s. It counts the number of leading wheels, the number of driving wheels powered by the engine, and the number of trailing wheels. The typical early American locomotive was classified as a 4-4-0.

The success of *Tom Thumb* and other steam locomotives made it clear that railroads were an economical, fast, and efficient way of moving freight. In 1840, there was 2,800 miles (4,500 kilometers) of track; that number would more than triple over the following decade, firmly establishing the importance of the railroad industry to America's future.

Stagecoaches

Stagecoaches were a cross between a horse-drawn taxi, a mail truck, and a money vault on wheels. The stagecoach was designed to carry up to twelve passengers squeezed inside the cabin. Riders sometimes perched on the roof, too. It also carried luggage, mail, money, and goods such as housewares to western territories. The stagecoach was pulled by four or six horses, which were traded for a fresh team at stations along the route.

There were three classes of travel: first, second, and third class. First-class passengers got to ride inside the coach for the entire journey. Second-class passengers were required to get out and walk when the road got particularly bad. And third-class passengers might have to help push the coach if it encountered a steep hill.

Traveling by stagecoach could be dangerous. The coaches were popular targets for bandits, who would steal passengers' valuables. They would even take the horses, leaving everyone stranded, often many miles from the nearest stop.

The most famous stagecoaches were those used by Wells, Fargo and Company, which owned the largest fleet in the world. They transported people as well as gold, money, and other valuable goods. The company also established twice-weekly mail service between St. Louis and San Francisco. Stagecoaches were eventually phased out as commercial vehicles in the early 1900s. They remain a stirring image of America's westward expansion.

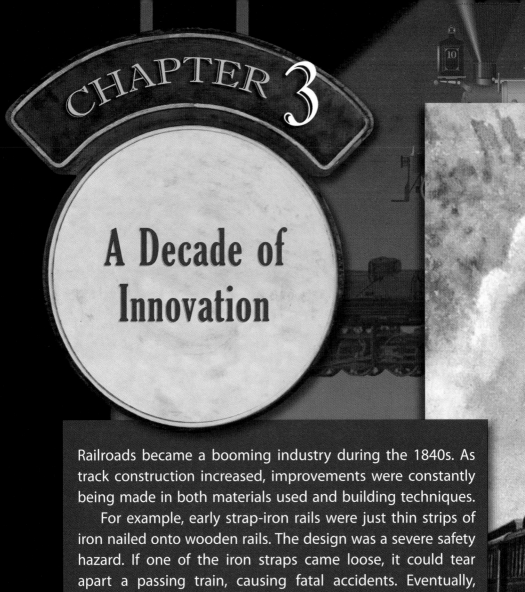

CHAPTER 3

A Decade of Innovation

Railroads became a booming industry during the 1840s. As track construction increased, improvements were constantly being made in both materials used and building techniques.

For example, early strap-iron rails were just thin strips of iron nailed onto wooden rails. The design was a severe safety hazard. If one of the iron straps came loose, it could tear apart a passing train, causing fatal accidents. Eventually, T-shaped iron rails were introduced. They distributed the weight of trains evenly and attached to the wooden crossties with a metal spike—a design still used today. The need for stronger materials also led to the development of better quality iron and steel.

The railroad industry impacted nearly every aspect of life in the growing United States. The concept of time zones was established by the railroads. Prior to the late 1800s, every city and town across America had its own time, determined by the sun. When it was noon in Washington, D.C., it was 12:12

Popular stories say New York Central's *No. 999* was the first steam locomotive to break the 100 mph (161 km/h) barrier in 1893. Some experts today say inaccurate timekeeping led to the claim and that *No. 999* didn't exceed 82 mph (132 km/h).

p.m. in New York City. Between Maine and California, travelers had to change their watches twenty times. This changed in 1883 when a group of railroad officers met and established a plan for five time zones—four in the United States and one in eastern Canada. The Standard Time Act was passed in 1918.

To keep trains on schedule, paying attention to the time was essential. Every station had a clock and this drove home the importance of timekeeping to the public.

Railroads were also closely linked with what was an exciting new way to communicate in the mid-1800s: the telegraph. Samuel Morse tirelessly petitioned the U.S. government to back his plan for a commercially useful telegraph system. It was finally approved by

In addition to inventing the telegraph (pictured above) and Morse code, Samuel Morse studied painting after graduating from college. Later in life, he became a well-known portrait artist.

Congress in 1844, and an experimental line was strung between Baltimore and Washington, D.C., along the B&O's right-of-way. The railroad agreed to share as long as it had free use of the new technology.

The success of using Morse code to send messages along a wire was proven, and one of the biggest roadblocks was solved. Setting up new lines cost an average of $150 a mile—a lot of money in those days. That price didn't include land rights, which were needed so that poles could be sunk and telegraph wire strung along them.

The first line proved that the answer was railroads, and most telegraph lines were set up along railroads after that, including along the tracks of the Delaware and Hudson Canal Company. An added benefit was that regular roads were often rutted, muddy, and hard to travel, but railroads offered easy access for installation and repairs of the telegraph system.

Putting People to Work

Railroads accounted for a wide variety of jobs. In addition to those working on the trains, the engineers and mechanics building and maintaining the locomotives, and the laborers laying the tracks, there were also jobs for selling tickets, handling freight paperwork, and managing the schedules, among many others. The railroads are credited with creating the country's first white-collar working class.

Building railroads was very expensive, and the federal government did not directly finance the industry. It did help indirectly through land grants, which let railroads use government-owned land free of charge. The government had a good reason for doing this. Once a railroad was operational and towns were established along the line, the government could sell the land for a much higher price. In general, railroads increased the real estate value of the surrounding area.

America's agriculture industry benefited greatly from the railroads. Farmers who once sold their crops only in their local communities now had access to a national market. Railroads also increased the farmers' profits because they could ship their goods for up to eighty percent

Railroads enabled farmers to sell more of their goods in more communities, resulting in larger farms and more jobs.

less than what it cost them to use wagons and steamships. Their goods got to market faster, too, so there was less chance of produce going bad. The higher income gave farmers more money to invest back into their farms.

Railroads often sold their land grants as farming acreage. Trains could then bring in farm machinery such as plows and reapers. They transported the building supplies, food, and goods needed to support the hundreds of towns springing up along the rails. And they brought people: businessmen, entrepreneurs, adventurers, and those looking for a fresh start in a new place. As more people moved westward toward the Mississippi River and beyond, the railroad industry continued to grow.

In fact, many consider the railroad industry to be the United States' first big business. It was much more than just transportation. The industry would provide hundreds of thousands of jobs directly and was integral to many other businesses that relied on the transport of their products. As the 1840s drew to a close, railroads were poised to expand even more.

Railroad Bridges

A Maryland bridge used by the B&O

One of the challenges to establishing a national railroad network was getting the trains over rivers, gullies, swamps, and other hard-to-cross places. To solve the problem, engineers built hundreds of bridges designed to support the weight of trains. These bridges were made of stone, concrete, steel, or timber, depending on the type of bridge.

The earliest railroad bridges in the United States were constructed from stone and were mostly located on the East Coast. Many of these bridges are still standing. Later, most bridges were built using iron and steel. The general types of bridges were, and are, truss, beam, girder, and span bridges.

In the early days of the railroad, the most common was a truss bridge. In engineering, a truss is a framework built to transfer the weight it is carrying to its supports. There are many types of truss bridges because the engineers patented their designs. One of the earliest was the Bollman iron suspension truss, developed by Wendel Bollman. While fine for the early locomotives, these bridges quickly became antiquated. There is only one Bollman truss railroad bridge left in existence. The 160-foot (49-meter) bridge is located in Savage, Maryland.

However, James Warren's truss, also known as the triangular truss, did endure. In his design, which he patented in 1848, the beams are positioned in a series of triangular sections. These help spread out the load on a bridge, letting it hold more weight and span farther than bridges using earlier designs.

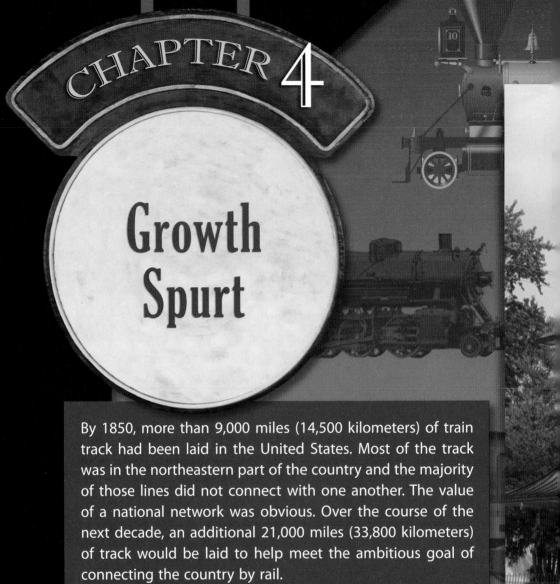

CHAPTER 4

Growth Spurt

By 1850, more than 9,000 miles (14,500 kilometers) of train track had been laid in the United States. Most of the track was in the northeastern part of the country and the majority of those lines did not connect with one another. The value of a national network was obvious. Over the course of the next decade, an additional 21,000 miles (33,800 kilometers) of track would be laid to help meet the ambitious goal of connecting the country by rail.

As an added incentive, the United States government granted six square miles (fifteen square kilometers) of federal land to railroad companies for every one mile (1.6 kilometers) of track they built. This policy played a big role in the growth of the rail industry. One of the first companies to benefit from the new law was the Illinois Central Railroad, which received a land grant of several million acres.

The land was not given in continuous chunks. Instead, the government distributed the land in alternating lots

The Illinois Central Railroad depot in the Galena Historic District was the station from which Ulysses S. Grant took a train to Washington, D.C., after he was elected as the eighteenth President of the United States.

along the path of the proposed railway. So for example, the railroad company would get lots one, three, five, seven, and nine, while the government kept lots two, four, six, eight, and ten. Once the track was laid and the railroad became operational, the value of all the land along the track would skyrocket. Railroad companies often sold their lots as soon as the rail was laid and used the money to finance more expansion. Sometimes they held on to the land and waited for it to become even more valuable. The government also benefited by owning land that was worth significantly more than before the railroad was built.

The land grant policy connected rail construction with real estate sales. Railroads would advertise—in America and Europe—the land they wanted to sell. The ads attracted settlers looking to build homes or businesses. These land sales increased immigration to the United States and encouraged western migration.

Between 1850 and 1870, the federal government granted nearly 130 million acres of land to the railroad industry, the majority of it west of the Mississippi River. That meant roughly seven percent of the country—real estate worth billions of dollars—was in the hands of around eighty railroad companies.

The land sales alone made many railroad executives millionaires, and very politically influential. They also made the railroad industry one of the most powerful and wealthy in the country, and one of the biggest employers. In return, the railroads connected the East Coast with the rest of the country, and shipping costs plummeted, letting small businesses prosper. The new settlements springing up along the railroads created jobs and business opportunities.

During the 1850s, many important rail connections were completed. New York City had access to the Great Lakes through the Erie Railroad and the New York Central Railroad. A railroad was constructed between Philadelphia and Pittsburgh. The B&O's line out of Baltimore reached the Ohio River in Virginia (that part of the state became West Virginia during the Civil War).

Ad from the Burlington and Missouri River Railroad Company, 1872

The *Pioneer*

Although the lion's share of tracks was laid in New England and other eastern areas, the Midwest also began to see significant growth. Chicago's first locomotive, the *Pioneer*, steamed along the newly laid tracks of the Galena and Chicago Union Railroad in 1848. The Illinois Central Railroad boomed in the 1850s, creating a route that ran the length of the state from Chicago in the north to Cairo in the south, at the meeting point of the Mississippi and Ohio rivers. Other carriers were also building tracks in the Midwest. In 1852, the Michigan Central and the Michigan Southern lines pushed in from the East. Both lines were later acquired by the New York Central system.

Prior to railroads, traveling to the Midwest meant taking a boat down the Ohio and Mississippi rivers. Railroads were much more direct. Chicago's location on Lake Michigan made it the perfect hub for the fertile Midwest, where farmers were flocking to grow crops and raise livestock.

By the eve of the Civil War, Chicago had eleven railroads and was considered the railroad center of the United States. As a result, it became an important trade center, and later a manufacturing center. The city's stockyards, where cows, pigs, and other animals were butchered and prepared for sale, became America's largest meatpacking center.

Railroads were also being built from the far bank of the Mississippi River westward. In December 1852, the Pacific Railroad extended five miles (eight kilometers) west from St. Louis. Four years later, the first railroad bridge across the Mississippi was opened between Rock Island, Illinois, and Davenport, Iowa. The Government Bridge let people living in eastern Iowa take a train over the Mississippi and on to their final destination of New York City in less than two days.

The Government Bridge, also know as Arsenal Bridge, connects Illinois and Iowa. It is one of the oldest bridges of its kind still in use on the Mississippi River.

The first steam locomotive on the Mohawk and Hudson Railroad

Even though the railroad industry was young, the 1850s saw considerable consolidation through mergers and acquisitions. For example, New York's first railroad, the Mohawk and Hudson, merged with a number of other lines to become the New York Central Railroad in 1853. It became one of the largest rail companies on the East Coast.

Railroads were being built throughout the United States, but the North far outpaced the South, which was mostly an agricultural region. About eighty percent of the country's manufacturing, which had prompted the rise of railroads, was located in the North.

One of the South's most notable lines, the Memphis and Charleston Railroad, was completed in 1857. It ran from Charleston, South Carolina, on the Atlantic Ocean, through Savannah, Georgia, to Memphis, Tennessee, on the Mississippi River.

Ten years later, the South's lack of an expansive railroad network would play a major role in its defeat by the North in the Civil War. The North's better railroad network made it easier to move troops and supplies, and that was critical to its success.

Train Stations

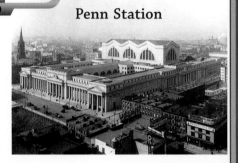

Penn Station

As the number of rail lines increased, so did the number of train stations, or depots. Even the smallest towns had stations. There were different types of depots. Some were small, simple buildings. Some were just repurposed boxcars. Many stations were elaborate structures. The size and services offered depended on the purpose the station and the size of the community it served.

Some depots were intended to serve travelers, some were used as storage places for freight, and others did both. The most basic station was usually little more than a covered platform.

Larger stations would be staffed by a railroad employee and usually had an indoor space for travelers and their baggage, an area to store freight, and a small office for the employee. If the station was in a remote area, it often had a living space for the employee.

Bigger towns sometimes had one station for passengers and a separate one for freight. As the industry grew, train stations became more elaborate and were constructed with expensive materials such as marble. As a result, many depots from the early twentieth century are still preserved.

Perhaps the most famous depot was the original Pennsylvania Station in New York City, which opened in 1910. Covering two city blocks, the building was designed by the famous architectural company McKim, Mead, and White. Constructed of pink marble and adorned with more than eighty columns, the station was meant to reflect the grandeur of the railroad. For many years, Penn Station was the busiest passenger-train hub in the United States, but after the advent of commercial airlines, train travel fell out of favor and the station became rundown from neglect. It was torn down in 1963 to make way for the construction of Madison Square Garden.

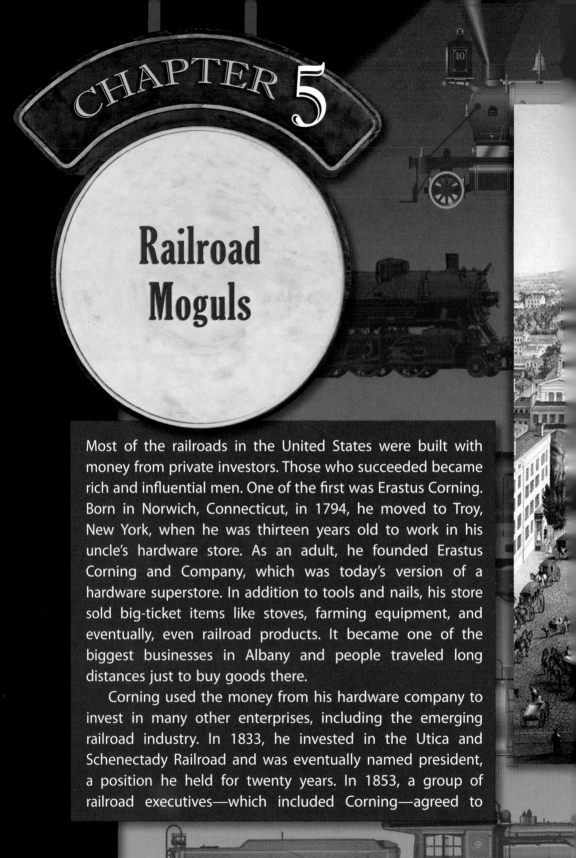

CHAPTER 5

Railroad Moguls

Most of the railroads in the United States were built with money from private investors. Those who succeeded became rich and influential men. One of the first was Erastus Corning. Born in Norwich, Connecticut, in 1794, he moved to Troy, New York, when he was thirteen years old to work in his uncle's hardware store. As an adult, he founded Erastus Corning and Company, which was today's version of a hardware superstore. In addition to tools and nails, his store sold big-ticket items like stoves, farming equipment, and eventually, even railroad products. It became one of the biggest businesses in Albany and people traveled long distances just to buy goods there.

Corning used the money from his hardware company to invest in many other enterprises, including the emerging railroad industry. In 1833, he invested in the Utica and Schenectady Railroad and was eventually named president, a position he held for twenty years. In 1853, a group of railroad executives—which included Corning—agreed to

The locomotive *Lightning* was built for the Syracuse and Utica Railroad. In this scene, it is shown pulling eight-wheel passenger cars on the tracks in Utica about 1850.

Erastus Corning

consolidate their small lines to form the New York Central Railroad, which became one of the most important lines in the country with its connection to Chicago. Corning owned the majority of shares in the new railroad. He was elected president and he served until he was forced to resign in 1864 due to ill health.

Another early railroad pioneer was Dean Richmond, a Buffalo, New York, businessman who organized the Buffalo and Rochester Railroad. That rail line was one of those consolidated into the New York Central Railroad. Richmond served as vice president of the New York Central until taking over for Corning after he resigned in 1864. Richmond ran the company until his death two years later. He was buried about a mile from the New York Central's main line.

While wealthy men, Corning and Richmond's success was confined to one main rail line. Others approached the business more ambitiously. These tycoons were business visionaries who were instrumental in establishing the full potential of the railroad industry and making the United States into a world economic power. They were often vilified for putting the safety of their workers and passengers second behind profits.

Dean Richmond

The most famous of the railroad barons was Cornelius Vanderbilt, born on May 27, 1794, in Staten Island, New York. He was the fourth of nine children in a family of modest means. When Cornelius was eleven, he quit school to help his father, who was a farmer. To sell his produce, the elder Vanderbilt had to transport it by water from Staten Island to New York, so Cornelius learned how to sail a boat. When he was sixteen, according to one story, Cornelius persuaded his mother to pay him $100 for plowing a rocky field so he could buy his own sailboat. He used it to begin a ferry service carrying passengers and freight between Staten Island and New York. Within two years, he had paid his mother back, with interest, and bought more sailboats.

His business strategy was to offer good service for a lower price than his competitors. During the War of 1812, the eighteen-year-old Vanderbilt was hired by the federal government to supply several forts in the region. During the war the British blockaded New York City. Seeing an opportunity, Vanderbilt brought food to New York City from farms along the Hudson River.

Cornelius Vanderbilt

Robert Livingston

After the war, he transported food, oil, and other goods between the Chesapeake Bay and New York. The profits from his business let him build a schooner and buy two more ships for handling his coastal trade. By 1817, he had saved up more than $9,000.

When he was twenty-four, Vanderbilt sold his sailing vessels to invest in steamboats, correctly guessing that they were the future of freight shipping. He was hired by Thomas Gibbons to captain a steamboat on the Hudson River between New York City and New Brunswick, New Jersey.

At the time, Gibbons was fighting a monopoly on Hudson River steamboats that had been granted by the New York legislature to Robert Livingston and Robert Fulton. By the time Gibbons hired Vanderbilt, Livingston and Fulton had died, but their heirs were still clinging tightly to the monopoly they had been granted.

Gibbons was sued for violating the monopoly and he fought back. The case eventually went to the Supreme

Robert Fulton

The steamboat *Cornelius Vanderbilt* raced the *Oregon* on the Hudson River in 1847. Vanderbilt captained the steamboat named after himself, and lost the race and his $1,000 bet with the captain of the *Oregon*. This painting may have been commissioned by Vanderbilt. It shows his ship in the lead and only the prow of the *Oregon*.

Court, which ruled in Gibbons's favor. Between helping Gibbons fight the monopoly, and captaining his ferry smoothly to earn the company a profit, Vanderbilt learned valuable lessons about how to run a business. He earned the nickname "the Commodore" for his cutthroat approach to business and his rough-and-tumble manners.

Vanderbilt started his own company and by the 1840s, he owned more than a hundred steamboats. At the time, his company employed more workers than any other in the United States.

He remained a driven businessman all his life. In his late sixties, he saw the opportunity that railroads provided, and he decided to get into the business. His first deal was to buy the New York and Harlem Railroad. He then purchased the Hudson River Railroad, and later the New York Central Railroad. With his son William, the Commodore bought and consolidated many East Coast railroad companies. William convinced his father to expand their holdings to Chicago so they bought the Lake Shore and Michigan Southern Railway, the Canada

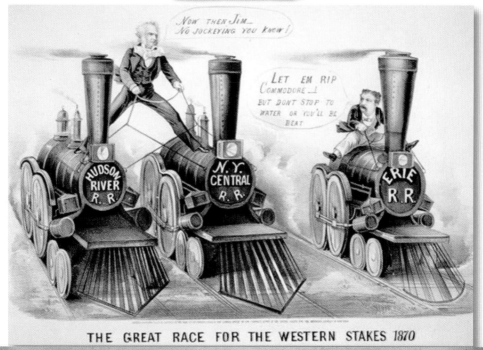

THE GREAT RACE FOR THE WESTERN STAKES 1870

Cornelius Vanderbilt entered the railroad business in 1857 and in little over a decade owned numerous railroads. In this cartoon, he's shown battling with competitor James Fisk for control of New York's rails.

Southern Railway, and the Michigan Central Railroad. These purchases created the largest rail system in the United States.

When he died at the age of eighty-two in 1877, Vanderbilt had amassed an estimated $100 million fortune; this was during a time when $100,000 was more than enough to make a person comfortable for life. In addition to his railroad and steamship empires, Vanderbilt is remembered for building Grand Central Terminal in 1871, which is a reminder of the golden age of the railroad industry and its lasting influence on American culture.

Steamships

Steamboat *Natchez*

Although often overshadowed by railroads, steamboats also played an integral role in establishing the United States as a global economic power. Steamboats were particularly important along the Mississippi River and its tributaries because they provided a means for the large-scale transportation of passengers and freight up and down the river. Steamboats were designed to be able to navigate in shallow water and the steam used to power the boats enabled them to travel upriver against the current. Steamboats helped make St. Louis the second largest port in the United States in the 1850s.

A typical steamboat was made of wood and ranged from 80 to 140 feet (24 to 43 meters) in length. Depending on the owner's budget, they could come with no frills or be ornate, with expensive furniture and fixtures. The boilers, which burned wood, were positioned toward the front to balance the weight of the cargo and passengers. The shelf life of steamboats was short. Usually after just five years the wood began to break down. Many steamships suffered damage or destruction from boilers exploding and from crashing into other ships.

Railroads eventually became the primary mode of transportation for passengers, but steamboats continued to be an important part of commerce along the Mississippi River well into the early twentieth century. The first steamboats could take three weeks to travel up the Mississippi to the Ohio River, but later models made the trip in four days.

1803   The Louisiana Purchase doubles the size of the United States.

1826   The Granite Railway opens in Massachusetts, and goes on to become one of the nation's first common carriers.

1830   Peter Cooper demonstrates the *Tom Thumb*.

1844   The first telegraph message is sent by Samuel Morse

1845   Texas becomes the twenty-eighth state.

1846   The United States goes to war with Mexico.

1848   The Treaty of Guadalupe Hidalgo is signed, ending the Mexican-American War; a survey of the boundary between Mexico and the United States begins and lasts for the next seven years. Gold is discovered in California. The *Pioneer* locomotive runs on Chicago's first railroad, the Galena and Chicago Union. James Warren patents his truss bridge.

1850   The Illinois Central Railroad receives a land grant of several million acres from the federal government. From 1850 to 1871, roughly 18,700 miles (30,100 kilometers) of track are laid by railroad companies that have received land grants.

1852   Railroads open routes from New York to Chicago.

1853   The New York Central Railroad is organized.

1854   Congress orders the Corps of Topographical Engineers to survey possible routes for a transcontinental railroad.

1856   The first railroad bridge across the Mississippi River is completed.

1857   The Memphis and Charleston Railroad is completed.

1862   Abraham Lincoln signs the first Pacific Railroad Act, which authorizes construction of a transcontinental railroad.

1869   George Westinghouse introduces air brakes for trains.

1871   Cornelius Vanderbilt builds Grand Central Terminal.

1918   The Standard Time Act is passed.

Chapter Notes

Chapter 1. Continental Expansion

1. Brigham D. Madsen, "John Williams Gunnison," *Utah History Encyclopedia,* http://www.media.utah.edu/UHE/index_frame.html

Chapter 2. A Transportation Revolution

1. Henry J. Sage, "The John Quincy Adams Years and the American Economy," Academic American History, May 27, 2010, http://www.academicamerican.com/jeffersonjackson/topics/jqadams_americaneconomy.html

Chapter 3. A Decade of Innovation

1. J.A.L. Waddell, *Bridge Engineering* (New York: John Wiley & Sons, 1916), p. 472.

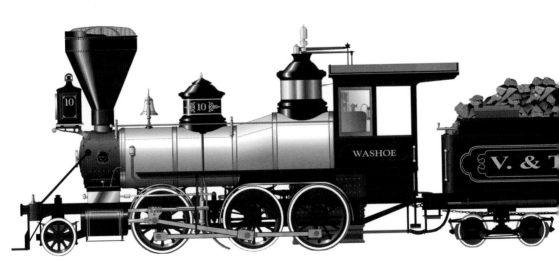

Ambrose, Stephen E. *Nothing Like It in the World: The Men Who Built the Transcontinental Railroad, 1863–1869*. New York: Simon & Schuster, 2000.

American-Rails.com "Railroad History, An Overview of the Past," http://www.american-rails.com/railroad-history.html

Bain, David H. *Empire Express: Building the First Transcontinental Railroad*. New York: Penguin, 1999

Beers, Henry P. "A History of the U.S. Topographical Engineers, 1818–1863," *The Military Engineer*, June 1942, http://www.topogs.org/History.htm

Benn, Bryan. "Which Was the World's First Genuine 100 mph Steam Locomotive?: New York Central & Hudson River 4-4-0 No. 999," http://www.germansteam.co.uk/tonup/tonup.html#NYC999

Evans, Richard T. and Helen M. Frye. "History of the Topographic Branch (Division)," United States Geographic Survey, http://pubs.usgs.gov/circ/1341/

Faith, Nicholas. *The World the Railways Made*, New York: Carroll & Graf, 1991.

Fisher, Kenneth L. *100 Minds That Made the Market*. New York: McGraw Hill, 1963.

Hastings, Paul. *Railroads: An International History*. London: Benn, 1972

Josephson, Matthew. *The Robber Barons*. New York: Mariner Books, 1962.

Licht, Walter. *Working for the Railroad: The Organization of Work in the Nineteenth Century*. New Jersey: Princeton University Press, 1967.

Pullman-Car.com, "George Pullman," http://www.pullman-car.com/history/george_pullman.html

Waddell, J.A.L. *Bridge Engineering*. New York: John Wiley & Sons, 1916.

Books

Lader, Curt. *Painless American History.* Hauppauge, NY: Barron's Educational Series, 2009.

Sammons, Sandra W. *The Two Henrys: Henry Plant and Henry Flagler and Their Railroads.* Sarasota, FL: Pineapple Press, 2010.

Smith, Robert W. *Spotlight on America: Industrial Revolution.* Westminster, CA: Teacher Created Resources, 2006

Williams, Harriet. *Road and Rail Transportation (History of Invention).* New York: Facts on File Publications, 2004.

Wilson, Jeff. *The Model Railroader's Guide to Industries Along the Tracks.* Circle Waukesha, WI: Kalmbach Publishing Company, 2004.

On the Internet

U.S. Corps of Topographical Engineers
http://www.topogs.org/History.htm

Travel Through Time: Train and Railroad History for Kids
http://www.travelproducts.com/resources/
train-and-railroad-history-for-kids/

Railroad Parts: History for Kids
http://www.partsgeek.com/brands/railroad_parts_history_for_kids.
html

All about Trains! A Children's Guide
http://trainhornsdelivered.com/allabtrchgu.html

Railroad Maps: 1828–1900
http://memory.loc.gov/ammem/gmdhtml/rrhtml/rrhome.html

Big Apple History: The Robber Barons
http://pbskids.org/bigapplehistory/business/topic8.html

cylinder (SIL-uhn-dur)— In a steam engine, a tube-shaped chamber that contains a piston, which is a disk that fits tightly inside the cylinder and moves up and down when pushed by a liquid or gas

driving wheels—Powered wheels driven by the locomotive's engine.

efficient (uh-FISH-uhnt)—Something that works well and doesn't waste energy.

engineer (en-juh-NEER)—A person who designs and builds engines, machines, or public works. On a train, the engineer is the driver.

excursion (ex-KUR-zhuhn)—A journey, or trip.

freight (FRAYT)—Goods carried by trains, ships, trucks, or planes. **excursion** (ex-KUR-zhuhn)—A journey, or trip.

gauge (GAGE)—The distance between the rails in a railroad track.

leading wheels—Unpowered wheels located in front of the driving wheels

legislature (LEJ-iss-lay-chur)—A group of people with the power to make or change laws.

locomotive (loh-kuh-MOH-tiv)—An engine used to pull railroad cars.

monopoly (muh-NOP-oh-lee)—The exclusive control of the supply or trade of goods or services.

Morse code (MORS code)—A code where letters are represented by combinations of long and short signals of sound or light.

piston (PISS-tun)—A disk that fits tightly inside a cylinder and moves up and down when pushed by a liquid or gas.

telegraph (TEL-uh-graf)—A system for sending messages over wire.

trailing wheels—Unpowered wheels behind the driving wheels

tycoon (TIE-koon)—An exceptionally wealthy and powerful businessperson.

venomous (VEH-num-uhss)—Capable of injecting poisonous fluid by means of a bite or sing.

ABOUT THE
AUTHOR

Kathleen Tracy has been a journalist for over twenty years. Her writing has been featured in magazines including *The Toronto Star's* "Star Week," *A&E Biography* magazine, *KidScreen,* and *TV Times.* She is also the author of numerous books for Mitchell Lane Publishers, including *We Visit Cuba; The Fall of the Berlin Wall;* and *The Story of September 11, 2001.* She lives in Southern California with her two dogs and African gray parrot.